Short
Or
Tall
Doesn't Matter At All!

Asaf Rozanes

This book belongs to

_____

MINDFUL MIA CLUB

Join the *Mindful Mia Club*!

Our amazing members take an active part in the book writing process and are an important part of our worldwide family!

Members also get FREE coloring pages, books and members only promotions.

https://mindful-mia.com/subscribe

To my Mia
the passion, light and power behind everything I do

Not too far away from here, in a small town,

There lived a little girl, who never frowned.

Mia always wanted to play,

She was the highlight of everyone's day.

Mia was just like all the other kids,

She was a regular girl, except for a few bits.

The other kids at school were tall,

And she was different from them all.

Mia studied hard, and was one of the best,

But she was shorter than the rest.

Mia's classmates laughed and mocked her almost every day, they were never careful of what they say.

That often made Mia sad,
So she decided to tell her dad.

He knew she didn't have to worry,
So he told her a story.

"At noon, the sun was being mean,"

"He said he was the tallest thing anyone has ever seen."

"He said to the moon, I'm taller than you,"

"You'll never be as tall as me; you know that's true."

"But time went by,"

"And at sunset, the sun wasn't that high."

"The moon told him he shouldn't boast,"

"Because it doesn't matter who's the tallest or knows the most."

"It's important to be friendly and nice,"

"They became friends and the Sun took her advice."

Mia learned to be good and polite,

She understood there were things more important

than height.

During break, the next day,

All the kids went out to play.

They wanted to play basketball,

But they didn't invite Mia, because she was small.

One of the kids threw the ball, and it started to roll,
It rolled away and fell in a small hole.

The kids couldn't reach it, but everyone wanted to
try, they would just hit their head and cry.

All of them took a turn, but they were too tall,
The kids needed someone brave, skinny and small.

Mia saw them scratching their heads and wandering about, She wanted to help, and get their ball out.

The little girl got the ball; she squeezed through, They cheered and said, "Mia, do you want to play too?"

The kids were amazed by her dribble and aim,
So, she showed them some moves they could use in the game.

The children were all very happy and excited,
To have such a good friend; they were indeed delighted.

They didn't care that Mia was short,
They were very happy to have someone to have fun with, help and support.
Mia was such a good friend, they would have never guessed,
That is why having a big heart is the best.

Friends are friends; whether you're big or small,
They will always be there for you to call.

Because at the end of the day, being short or tall,
As even the Sun and the Moon now know...
It just doesn't matter at all!

Mia and Dad sprinkled and scattered love all over this book!

Were you able to notice and find all the heart shapes we scattered around?

Spoiler Alert:

The next page contains all the hidden locations, flip the page at your own risk ☺

Pssst...Here's where we hid the heart shapes:

Page 5:
On the Tree trunk

Page 7:
On the back of the brown teacher's desk

Page 9:
On the bottle on the shelf

Page 15:
On the bottom of the rock which the red shirted boy is climbing on

Page 17:
On the backboard of the basket board

Page 23:
On the left side of the fence, within the grass

Help us Make a Difference

Thank you for purchasing our book and joining us on our *important* mission to ***empower children and parents*** all over the world!

If you enjoyed reading this book, we would love to read your honest review.

Reviews help us tremendously as they get our books noticed so we can continue our mission to empower more children and parents around the world!

Thank You!

Mia & Dad

Mia and Dad just LOVE to color and we're sure you do too!

So, we've added a few of our early book sketches just for you to color in any way you like.

Make the sky pink and the grass blue, it's all up to you!

More books by Asaf Rozanes

*Mindful Mia - **Award-Winning Children Empowering** book series*

Short Or Tall Doesn't Matter At All
(Mindful Mia, Book #1)

Through an inspiring tale about the sun and the moon and how everyone, no matter how different they are has unique traits and skills, this real life story shows parents and kids alike what is really important in life - like having a good heart and turning bullying into new friendships.

Tomorrow Is Near, But Today Is Here
(Mindful Mia, Book #2)

The stress, worry and anxiety our children face is greater than any generation before. I wrote this book to assist my daughter with anxiety and her worries: have a positive perspective on experiencing and enjoying life and what it may bring. Surprisingly this also drastically reduced the time it now takes her to fall asleep.

Part Of The Rainbow (Mindful Mia, Book #3)

In this witty and colorful tale, Mia arrives at the first day of school and is shocked to her green whiskers by what she experiences there and how it would change her life forever!

The Monster Friend (Mindful Mia, Book #4)

Monsters are REAL! It's time to stop ignoring their existence and start to get to know them and why they came to pay us a visit. Join Mia in this inspiring tale about confronting your fears.

The Feelings Library (Mindful Mia, Book #5)

There are no bad feelings, we should learn to experience all our feelings - from happiness to anger - to find what they teach us about the world, about others, about our thoughts but mostly about us.

More books by Asaf Rozanes

Fairy Fights

Losing your first tooth can be scary. But Mia and a pair of fairies make it fun! Read Fairy Fights, and soothe your child's fears today!

Staying At Home

This book was written for days like today - Whether you're sick, in quarantine or at home have to stay. A funny and inspiring book to help spend your long times at home in a fun and productive way!

CPSIA information can be obtained
at www.ICGtesting.com
Printed in the USA
LVHW072231101121
703034LV00006B/47